International Baccalaureate
Computer Science
HL & SL
TOPIC 3: NETWORKS

Sarah Shakibi PhD

Contents

Introduction

As with the other titles in this series of revision notes for the IB Computer Science syllabus I draw your attention to the 'verb' used in each specification point. This is important since it is the verb that determines the 'depth' to which you need to know any given topic.

Some topics lend themselves very well to becoming Potential Exam Questions and I've marked these as PEQ.

VERB	What you should do
Define	Give a short but *technically accurate* definition or meaning for what is asked.
Outline	Give a 'sketch' of the overall topic asked.
Explain	Give accurate and logically ordered explanation for what is asked.
Describe	Paint a broad picture of what is asked, putting in enough detail to make it technically accurate
Discuss	Consider two pros, two cons for what is asked. Explain them logically and in order. Draw an intelligent conclusion at the end.
Evaluate	Consider the 'value' of what is asked. Explain if it is of any value or not of any value.
PEQ	Potential Exam Question – learn well!

Networks - Definition

When two or more computers are **connected,** this creates a basic network. You will see many different types of network discussed in the various specification points which follow but for now just remember the most **basic network** is two computers connected to each other. This can be by using the most **basic hardware → a cable**:

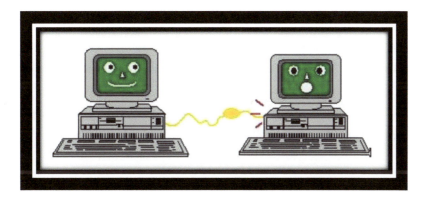

Why do we need networks?

Imagine sitting in a room with 20 computers in a school. Some of you are using files, some are browsing, some using email, some printing. It would be extremely difficult to do all these differenet jobs separately. So why not set up a network to allow:

- Sharing of files – from a file server
- Printing documents – from a print server → common printer
- Browsing the World Wide Web – a web server

A network has many uses and these are just some of the most common examples.

A computer network is a collection of computing devices that are connected in various ways to communicate and share resources

Usually, the connections between computers in a network are made using physical wires or cables. However, some connections are wireless, using radio waves or infrared signals to transmit data.

Computer networks contain devices other than computers. Printers, for instance, can be connected directly to a network so that anyone on the network can print to them. Networks also contain a ==variety of devices for handling network traffic==.

The generic term **node** or **host** to refer to any device on a network.

Types of Networks (Network topologies- configurations)

Computer networks can be classified in various ways. One method of categorising the different types of networks is by their scope or scale, and as such the "==area==" they cover. Consequently, and as a result of tradition, networks in this sense are called area networks. Other methods include the network configuration such as topology of area networks, for example ring, star, and bus configurations.

Basic Network Types

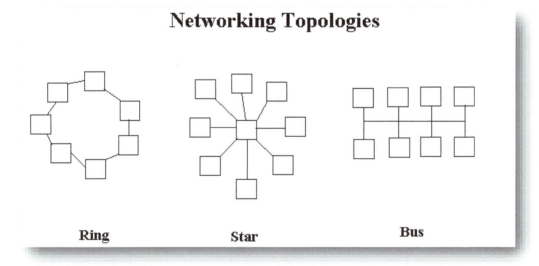

3.1.1 Identify different types of networks

Examples include local area network (LAN), virtual local area network (VLAN), wide area network (WAN), storage area network (SAN), wireless local area network (WLAN), internet, extranet, virtual private network (VPN), personal area network (PAN), peer-to-peer (P2P).

S/E, **INT** Globalization has been accelerated by the technical advances linked to network development. (topology: an area of pure mathematics that deals with the properties of surfaces/infrastructures

Local Area Network - LAN

Definition: A network over a small geographical distance – usually on one site and typically used by one organisation

- Short geographical distance
- Usually connected via cables due to the short distances
- Schools, homes, small offices
- Can be Star, Ring or Bus
- Most LANS are made up of one or more **servers (a high specification computer with sufficient processing power and storage capacity to service a number of users)** and **clients (any computer attached to the network)**

Virtual Local Area Network -VLAN

Definition: Virtual Local Area Networks allow getting rid of the limitations of physical architecture.

- A virtual local-area network is a network of computers that **behave as if they are connected to the same topology (eg all star shaped)**, but are actually physically located in different segments of a LAN.
- VLAN configurations are generally comprised and maintained via software rather than hardware hence the name 'virtual' because it's the software that is 'creating' the impression of a uniform topology.

- o This makes the network extremely flexible as it allows computers to be removed from the VLAN and located elsewhere without having to physically rewire the whole system to fit the new configuration.

Wide Area Network –WAN

Definition: A number of computers and peripherals (devices such as printers) connected together over a large geographical distance.

This means that the network extends beyond a **single site** and can be as large as the global network of networks ie the Internet.

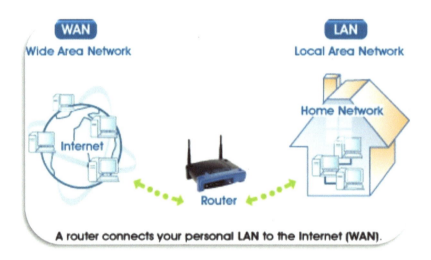

A router connects your personal LAN to the Internet (WAN).

- o A wide-area network (WAN) is a geographically-dispersed collection of two or more LANs.
- o A WAN permits communication among smaller networks eg in different parts of the same country or on different continents.
- o (Often one particular node (one single machine) on a LAN is set up to serve as a gateway to handle all communication going through that LAN and other networks.)

Storage Area Network- SAN

Definition: A **storage area network** is a secure high-speed data transfer **network** that provides access to consolidated block-level **storage**.

A **SAN** makes a **network** of **storage** devices accessible to multiple servers.

SAN devices appear to servers as attached drives, eliminating traditional **network** bottlenecks.

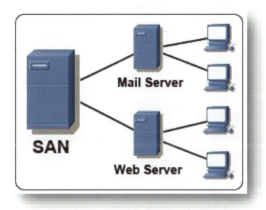

Wireless Local Area Network-WLAN

Definition: A LAN that does not use cables but connects using radio waves

WiFi is the generic term for a **Wireless Local Area Network or WLAN.** Devices can connect wirelessly to each other and a connection can be made to the Internet. WiFi operates to a generic standard called IEEE ensuring that all devices are compliant and can connect and transmit data around the network.

- o A WLAN in a home or office uses a wireless router that transmits a WiFi signal accessible within a few meters of the device.
- o WiFi **hotspots** are set up by telecommunication companies and use wireless routers to allow access over a larger distance – approximately 250 meters.

Virtual Private Network-VPN

Definition: **A** Virtual Private Networks, allow users to securely access a private network and share data remotely **through** public networks. It acts like a firewall by protecting the sharing of data **online.**

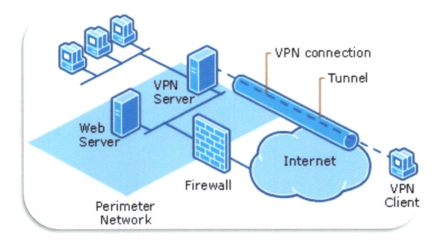

- o A VPN supports network connectivity over a **possibly long physical connection**.
- o <mark>Key feature of a VPN: ability to use ***public networks like the Internet*** rather than rely on very expensive private leased lines using a method called **<u>tunnelling</u>**, a VPN use the same hardware infrastructure as existing Internet or intranet links.</mark>

Peer-to-Peer Network - P2P

Definition: A network configuration where all devices in a network share resources between them rather than having a server.

Each workstation therefore can act either as a client or as the server, depending on the current task.

A mesh – P2P

- o   If all the computers in this configuration are connected to each other, it is called a **mesh**.

Personal Area Network – PAN

Definition: A PAN is a computer network created and organised around the needs of one individual person.

- It can consist of a mobile phone, a computer, and other devices which can communicate with each other via the PAN.
- It also allows connection to other networks and the Internet.
- PANs can be constructed using wireless technology or cables.

Open Systems

3.1.2 Outline the importance of standards in the construction of networks

> **INT** Standards enable compatibility through a common "language" internationally.

Standards or **protocols** exist for communication between networks. These are very important and need to exist in order to ensure that devices communicate with each other efficiently and without interfering with each other.

WiFi operates to IEEE 802.11 ensuring all devices are compliant and can connect and transmit data around the network.

A protocol called **Carrier Sense Multiple Access with Collision Avoidance (CSMA/CA)** was developed to enable various devices to transmit data at high speeds without interfering with each other.

3.1.3 Describe how communication over networks is broken down into different layers.

> Awareness of the OSI seven layer model is required, but an understanding of the functioning of each layer is not.

In order for Device A to be able to communicate with Device B, *irrespective* of where each of these devices is geographically there are **7 layers** of communication which need to be covered.

If Device A is on the left hand side and Device B is on the right and A sends something to B then we start at the top layer or Human level 7 on the left eg with a mail application.

Go down the layers on the left

Climb up the layers on the right.

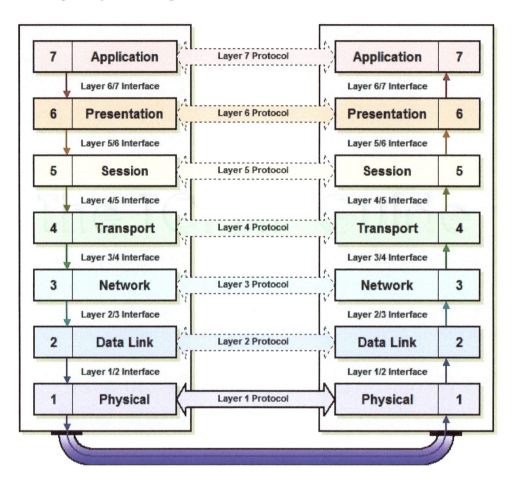

3.1.4 <u>Identify</u> the technologies required to provide a VPN

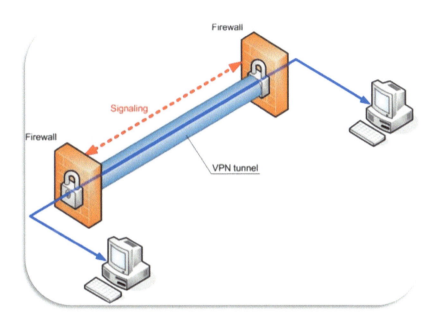

> Client VPN software to make a secure **remote connection.**

> VPN-aware **routers** and **firewalls** to permit legitimate VPN traffic to pass without being blocked

> VPN **server to handle and manage** incoming VPN traffic and to establish and manage VPN sessions and their access to network resources.

3.1.5 **Evaluate** the use of a VPN

> **S/E**, **AIM 9** The use of a VPN has led to changes in working patterns.

- A VPN is one solution to establishing long-distance and/or secured network connections.
- VPNs are normally deployed by businesses or organisations rather than by individuals, but virtual networks can be reached from inside a home network.

A VPN can save an organisation money in several situations:

- ➢ Eliminating the need for expensive long-distance leased lines because we can tunnel through the public network
- ➢ Reducing long-distance telephone charges (VoIP)
- ➢ Offloading support costs – no leased line support, no telephone line support required anylonger

Disadvantages:

- VPNs require detailed understanding of network security issues and careful installation / configuration to ensure sufficient protection on a public network like the Internet (the tunnel could be used by outside interceptors if not carefully planned)
- The reliability and performance of an Internet-based VPN is not under an organisation's direct control. It is only as good as it's ISP.
- Historically, VPN products and solutions from different vendors have not always been compatible due to issues with VPN technology standards. Attempting to mix and match equipment may cause technical problems, and using equipment from one provider may not give as great a cost savings.

Data transmission

Network Protocols

3.1.6 Define the terms: protocol, data packet

Definition: A protocol is a set of rules for interaction between two or more devices

One of the biggest problems with computer communications is getting the various computers, networks, and peripheral devices to talk to each other. There are so many different manufacturers of hardware and so many different ways of transmitting data that it is essential that there are accepted standards for data transmission.

Data:

Data is a meaningless stream of characters which are encoded in binary ie in the form suitable for use with a computer.

Data Packet

A packet is a collection of data that can be used by computers which need to communicate with each other, usually as part of a network. To improve communication performance and reliability(to economise on bandwidth), each message sent between two network devices is often divided into packets by the hardware and software.

Definition: A data packet is a basic unit of communication over a digital network. When data is to be transmitted across wired or wireless networks it is broken down into packets and then re-assembled upon reaching its destsination.

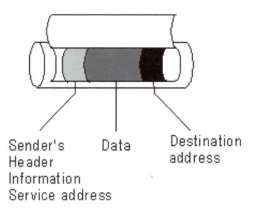

Sender's   Data   Destination
Header   address
Information
Service address

<mark>A data packet can be identified uniquely by its header and corresponding MAC address</mark> which identifies which network has initiated it and where the **final destination** is.

Data packets also preserve their order of placement inside a larger packet of transmitted data.

3.1.7 Explain why protocols are necessary.

Including data integrity, flow control, deadlock, congestion, error checking.

As explained in the previous section, one of the biggest problems with computer communications is getting the various computers, networks and peripheral devices to talk to each other smoothly, without interruption and most importantly without errors.

Protocols are a method of ensuring that different computers can communicate with each other.

A protocol is a set of rules. In the context of digital communications there are a number of rules that have been established in relation to the transmission of data.

Protocols cover the format in which data should be transmitted and how items of data are identified.

Data integrity: HTTPS protocol **is used for the protection of internet traffic, it assures about the** data integrity **and data protection.**

An outsider cannot intercept the data that transmitted via HTTPS.

SSL Protocol **establishes a secure connection between two servers or a customer's browser and the company's web server.**

 Data flow control: Flow control is the management of data flow between computers or devices or between nodes in a network so that the data can be handled at an efficient pace. Too much data arriving before a device can handle it causes data overflow, meaning the data is either lost or must be retransmitted.

For serial data transmission locally or in a network, the Xon/Xoff protocol can be used.

For modem connections, either Xon/Xoff or CTS/RTS (Clear to Send/Ready to Send) commands can be used to control data flow.

In a network, flow control can also be applied by refusing additional device connections until the flow of traffic has subsided.

Data deadlock: A **deadlock is a situation in which two computer programs sharing the same resource are effectively preventing each other from accessing the resource**, resulting in both programs ceasing to function. The earliest computer operating systems ran only one program at a time.

Data congestion: Network **congestion** in **data** networking and queueing theory is the reduced quality of service that occurs when a network node or link is carrying more **data** than it can handle. Typical effects include queueing delay, packet loss or the blocking of new connections.

Error checking protocols: various such protocols exist to ensure that data packets are sent correctly across from sender to receiver. Parity checks and majority voting are two examples of error checking protocols.

Parity check: counts the number of '1' bits in the message sent and compares with the number of '1's received to check of correct number have arrived. (referred to as Even/Odd parity)

Majority voting: sends each bit 3 times and then checks to see how many of those have arrived correctly. Eg if '0 is sent 3 times and arrives as '001' then because 2 out of 3 digits are 0 it is assumed that the sender has in fact send 0.

3.1.8 Explain why the speed of data transmission across a network can vary

All type of physical connections, be it digital subscriber line (DSL), cable modem, or even phone modems fall into the category of <mark>broadband</mark> connections. Depending on the location and whether access is by satellite, phone wire, video cable, or fiber optics, it is possible to obtain broadband transfer speeds that range from 384 kilobits per second to 1 gigabits per second. Increasingly more households are moving away from the use of phone modems to a broadband solution for their computing network needs. Debate between the DSL and cable modem communities continue to rage to see who can claim the dominant market share

3.1.9 Explain why compression of data is often necessary when transmitting across a network.

S/E, INT Compression has enabled information to be disseminated more rapidly.

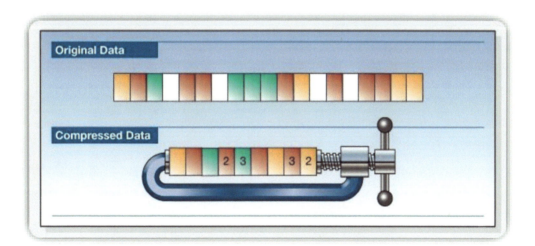

There are many circumstances under which files which are used to store data can become very large eg high resolution images or music sampled at a high frequency will produce files which can be several megabytes in size.

A full-length movie can take up several gigabytes of storage space.

In order to reduce storage requirements and make it quicker to transmit files we can use compression.

Compression is the process of reducing the number of bits required to represent data.

Two main techniques are:

- Lossless compression: the compressed file is as accurate as it was before compression – no data is lost.
- Lossy compression – there will be some degradation in the data, for example a grainier image.

Network Connections

3.1.10 Outline the characteristics of different transmission media

> Characteristics include: speed, reliability, cost and security.
>
> Transmission media include: metal conductor, fibre optic, wireless.

To improve the efficiency of transferring data over a shared communication line, messages are divided into fixed-size, numbered packets.

These packets are sent over the network individually to their destination, where they are collected and reassembled into the original message.

This approach is referred to as packet switching.

Fibre Optics

- Speed: Very good
- Cost: High
- Reliability: Good
- Security: Good

An optical fibre is a thin, flexible medium which conducts quick pulses of light which each represent one bit. Fibre optics can transfer hundreds of gigabits per second and can't take electromagnetic interference, making it the preferred choice of long-haul transmission media.

Twisted Pair (inexpensive/relatively slow/reliable/security relatively good)

- The twisted pair copper cables are the most inexpensive type of transmission media
- Reliable since has been in use for many years by phone companies
- Two copper wires are twisted together and coated with a protective layer.

Coaxial Cable

Like twisted pair, coaxial cable consists of two copper wires, but instead of being parallel, they are concentric. With the construction and special type of shielding and insulation, the coaxial cable can carry a lot more **bits much faster than the twisted pair.** Security (low/medium), cost (low/medium)

3.1.11 Explain how data is transmitted by packet switching

One of the methods used to send data across networks is called **packet switching.**

Data sent over the Internet are broken down into smaller chunks called **packets.** Each packet of data will contain additional information including

- a **packet sequence number**
- a **source address**
- a **destination address**
- a **checksum**

Packets of data are normally made up of:

Header :
<ul><li>**MAC address of sender & receiver**</li><li>**Sender & receiver IP address**</li><li>**Which protocol is used**</li><li>**Packet or sequence number**</li></ul>
Body: **The actual data themselves**
Footer: **A checksum**

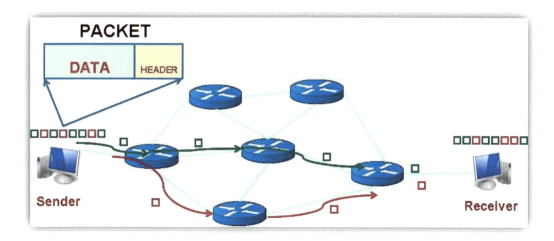

The packets are sent to their destination using the destination address.

Each packet may travel along a different route but they are **re-assembled** at the destination using the packet sequence numbers.

The **checksum** will identify any errors. It works by adding together the values of all the data held in a packet and transmitting those data along with the packet. This number is checked at the destination and if it is the same then the chances are that the data have been received correctly. If different, the packet is sent again.

Wireless networking

3.1.12 Outline the advantages and disadvantages of wireless networks

<u>PEQ</u>

> **S/E** wireless networks have led to changes in working patterns, social activities and raised health issues.

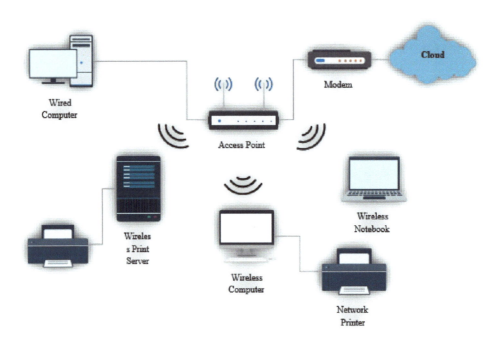

ADVANTAGES:

1. <mark>flexibility of their ad-hoc situation</mark> so workstations can be added as and when required,
2. the implementation <mark>cost is cheaper</mark> than wired network since it uses unlicensed radio spectrum
3. they are <mark>ideal for the non-reachable places</mark> such as across river or mountain or rural area,

4. ideal for temporary LAN network setups since it does not need cabling therefore no space or time required for laying cables
5. People can switch from router to router automatically depending in which connection is best
6. Follows global WiFi standards

DISADVANTAGES:

1. digital signals have to penetrate through the permeable air, there is a reduction in speed compared to wired networks,

2. they are less secure because cracker's laptop can act as access point. If you connected to their laptop, they'll read all your information sensitive information.

3. They are greatly affected by their surrounding and as a consequence signal strength affected by objects blocking its path, interference, and attenuation

4. WEP: this encryption is not difficult to hack and WPA2 has solved this problem

5. Easy to steal data from access points if they are available to intruders

3.1.13 Describe the hardware and software components of a wireless network.

The basic wireless, peer-to-peer network consists of these components:

Wireless router: The heart of the wireless network is the wireless router. Like a wire-based network, the hub is a central location that all computers connect to, providing the computers with network access.

The wireless hubs now available also serve as routers. They're also called *access points,* so get used to that term as well.

Despite the nomenclature confusion, all you need to know is that the hub/router/access point is a smart little beast that helps manage wireless connections and also helps connect your wireless network to the Internet.

Wire-based connections: Almost every wireless router has one or more standard, wire-based Ethernet port. One port is used to connect the router to a broadband modem. Other Ethernet ports might be also available, allowing you to connect standard wire-based networking to the wireless hub.

Wireless NIC: Your computer needs a wireless network information card, or NIC, to talk with the wireless router. A laptop comes standard with a wireless NIC, but for a desktop PC you have to get a wireless NIC as an option. It's installed internally as an expansion card, or you can use one of the various plug-in USB wireless NICs.

3.1.14 Describe the characteristics of wireless networks

Include: WiFi; Worldwide Interoperability for Microwave Access (WiMAX); 3G mobile; future networks.

S/E, **INT** Connectivity between different locations.

Wifi : Discussed in section 3.1.1

WiMAX:

- World wide interoperability for Microwave Access
- Based on the IEEE 802.16 standard
- Designed for creating Metropolitan Area Networks
- Similar to WiFi but with a much wider range of around 3000 square metres

1. Worldwide Interoperability for Microwave Access (WiMAX) "is a wireless communications standard designed to provide ==30 to 40 megabit-per-second data rates,==
2. WiMAX Forum describes it as " a standards-based technology enabling the delivery of last mile wireless broadband access as an alternative to cable and DSL "
3. ==WiMAX is a part of fourth generation wireless-communication technology (4G) and is able to cover a staggering radius of about 50 km.==

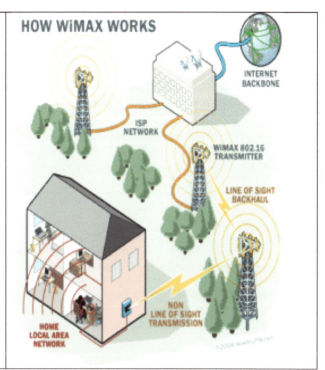

3G is able to deal with video and audio files for these devices.

It has a potential transfer speeds of up to 3 Mbps, in comparison to 2G's 144 Kbps.

Future Networks

LTE - It is part of the fourth generation wireless-communication technology and is only provided in a hand full of countries. It is theoretically capable of speeds of up to ==299.6 Mbps==

Network Security

3.1.15 Describe the different methods of network security PEQ

> Include encryption types, userID, trusted media access control (MAC) addresses.
>
> **S/E** Wireless networks have led to concerns about the security of the user's data.

Firewalls

A firewall is a hardware and software that serve as a special gateway to a network, protecting it from inappropriate access.

A firewall filters the network traffic that comes in, checking the validity of the messages as much as possible and perhaps denying some messages altogether.

The main goal of a firewall is to protect (and, to some extent, hide) a set of more loosely administered machines that reside "behind" it.

A firewall enforces an organisation's access control policy. For example, a particular organisation may allow network communication only between its users and the "outside world" via email, but deny other types of communication, such as accessing websites. Another organisation may allow its users to freely access the resources of the Internet, but may not want general Internet users to be able to infiltrate its systems or gain access to its data.

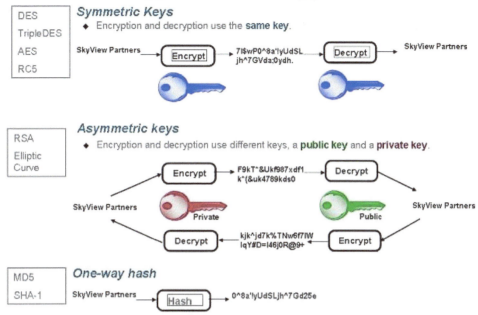

Wireless Encryption

WiFi Protected Access (WPA/WPA2) : a protocol for encrypting data and ensuring security on WiFi networks

MAC Address

Every piece of **hardware** on a network has a unique **MAC address**. This is embedded in the hardware when the product is made in the factory, and the user cannot change it.

On a computer, the MAC address is a unique code built into a NIC. No two computers have the same MAC address.

A MAC address is made up of 48 **bits** of data, usually written as 12 **hexadecimal** characters.

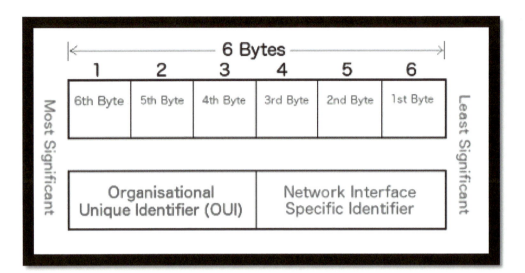

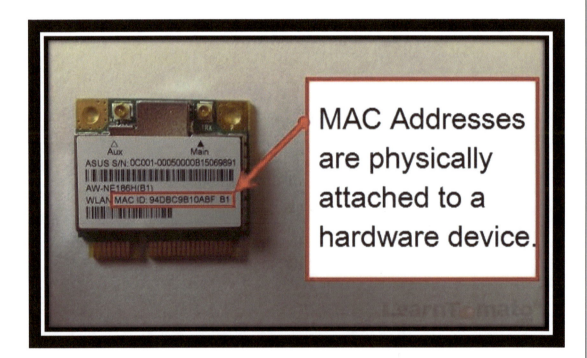

3.1.16 Evaluate the advantages and disadvantages of each method of network security.

Data Encryption

Encryption is the process of converting ordinary text, referred to as plaintext into a form that is unreadable, called cipher text.

In its simplest terms, such implementation allows users to encrypt their data using a key and send it along a network to another node, who has access to another key which can "unlock" said data.

This allows for a network-based security problem known as the "man-in-the-middle" attack to be circumvented.

Network communication goes through many locations and devices as it moves from its source to its destination, usually such communication is passed along as appropriate without a problem. A man-in-the-middle attack occurs when someone has access to the communication path at some point in the network and "listens," usually with the help of a program, to the traffic as it goes by. The goal is to intercept vital information, such as a password being transmitted as part of an email message. Encryption is a method of guarding against these problems.

One disadvantage that may exist with encryption lies with its implementation. Using complex algorithms to encrypt and decrypt data may prove slow and tedious to the ordinary end-user whose ultimate goal is to access resources from alternate nodes in a network. Consequently, encrypting and decrypting may take unwelcome time. Additionally, not all nodes may have the protocol to accept an encrypted stream of data, and as such may not know what to do with the data, and only accept plaintext. As a result, the client may have to transmit unprotected data as a result of another node's failure.

Firewalls

Advantages

1. Relatively <mark>inexpensive or free</mark> for personal use.

2. New releases are becoming user friendly.

3. <mark>Some</mark> firewalls but not all can <mark>detect viruses, worms, Trojan horses, or data collectors</mark>.

4. A firewall <mark>blocks</mark> evil packets from being permitted to reach a place where they can do harm.

Disadvantages

1. Firewalls evolve due to cracker's ability to circumvent the increases.

2. <mark>Firewalls cannot protect you from internal sabotage</mark> within a network or from allowing other user's access to your PC.

3. Firewalls offer weak defense from viruses.

"Putting asbestos around your computer isn't the same as installing a firewall."

http://communicrossings.com/safer-internet-connection-use-firewall

MAC address

Advantages

1. The advantage to MAC filtering is that there is no attachment cost to devices that connect to the network.
2. The policy is set on a router or switch, and the equipment attached either is permitted or it is not.
3. The person attaching the equipment has nothing to do.

Disadvantages

1. The disadvantage to MAC filtering is that it is easy to spoof.
2. Because of the broadcast nature of Ethernet, and particularly wireless Ethernet, an advisory can sit on the wire and just listen to traffic to and from permitted MAC addresses.
3. Then, the advisory can change his MAC address to a permitted one, and in most cases obtain access to the network.

http://www.glasbergen.com/ngg_tag/information-safe/nggallery/image/cartoons-about-data-security-protecting-data-sticky-notes-backing-up-computer-network-backup

References:

http://www.justanswer.com/mac-computers/34syh-advantages-disadvantage-using-mac-address.html

http://www.pinktec.ca/articles/firewalls_advantages.htm